Kozmic Dust

Traci Martin

India | USA | UK

Copyright © Traci Martin
All Rights Reserved.

This book has been self-published with all reasonable efforts taken to make the material error-free by the author. No part of this book shall be used, reproduced in any manner whatsoever without written permission from the author, except in the case of brief quotations embodied in critical articles and reviews.

The Author of this book is solely responsible and liable for its content including but not limited to the views, representations, descriptions, statements, information, opinions, and references ["Content"]. The Content of this book shall not constitute or be construed or deemed to reflect the opinion or expression of the Publisher or Editor. Neither the Publisher nor Editor endorse or approve the Content of this book or guarantee the reliability, accuracy, or completeness of the Content published herein and do not make any representations or warranties of any kind, express or implied, including but not limited to the implied warranties of merchantability, fitness for a particular purpose.

The Publisher and Editor shall not be liable whatsoever...

Made with ❤ on the BookLeaf Publishing Platform
www.bookleafpub.in
www.bookleafpub.com

Dedication

I dedicate this poetry book to my dad Marty Martin who always believed in me and supported my dreams. I also dedicate it to my daughter Mazzy Starr who is my reason for living and pursuing my dream of being a writer.

Preface

Acknowledgements

1. Rebirth

We're so few and far between.
Each living in our own world.
Thinking, breathing, eating and sleeping
All in different syncrasies..

Making our own direction in life,
Having our own personal influences,
We crave to have an inspiration.
A dream to catch, a star to become.

Friends... they come and go.
Here awhile then off again
To become the thing they craved the most,
To become themselves.

Eventually, you have to break free
To make your own reality
Become your own world
And live it as yourself.

37. Who's There?

The red eyed bandit is chasing us down
Paranoid spirits question every sound
For our soul he haunts until we are found
This red eyed bandit, have you seen him around?

In war our people will separate
While our government moves to set the date
In the back of their minds they start to create
Strategies of destructions in our fate.

Kindred spirits being sent away
Many being lost on that September day
It reminded us all to begin to pray
For the red eyed bandit is here to stay.

We look to the bible in time of need
Over population started with Adam and Eve
By turning those pages is it God you receive?
Or will the red eyed bandit win you over with greed?

If everything in life has a beginning and end
And if God created you and the rules that you bend
Your money made up is money you spend
On your ticket to heaven or this red eyed friend.

What will you do when the day is here?
War all around us I think it is near
Will you believe out of faith or believe out of fear?
You choose the one you wish to appear.

2. The Beaten Path

You asked me where I was, where I was in my spiritual walk.
I could take you on a journey of when I heard him start to talk.
I closed my eyes, I bowed my head, and opened up my mind.
He cleared a path that once was lost and now its mine to find.

He gives me clues along the way but let's me make the choice.
I pray for guidance, I pray for strength, I listen for his voice.
Not always making the right decisions, you live and learn they say.
All I do sometimes to get by is take it day by day.

I've been through many storms in life, left footprints in the sand.
Some battles that I went alone, I fell down now I stand.
I cannot change the past, for that time is gone in space.
Looking forward, looking ahead, my dreams I start to chase.

Maybe I regret some things but I never have objected.
Just learned a new way to look at life, I look now with perspective.
Like take the time I lost my mind, I was stuck inside my head.
Praying for a miracle while wishing I was dead.

The pain was so unbearable, scars to big to hide.
I couldn't have made it through this hell without him by my side.
Patiently I learned forgiveness while reading from his book.
No one will ever know just how much it was I took.

How much is was everyday to cover up the pain.
I always wonder if anyone else would have handled things the same.
None of us are broken even when we seem so weak.
We all go through these trials in life, each story is unique.

Sometimes we like to look back, on the past and who we were.
You have to take the good with bad and let the rest of it occur.
Deep down I've conquered fears in life, I've taken on abuse.

It's made me stronger, not going to lie, or use it as an excuse.

I put myself in these situations I couldn't see the light.
The only thing left for me to do, to get out I had to fight.
You only know one side of the story, you don't know the other half.
I learned to walk away from it all when I took the beaten path.

3. Child of God

If you only knew the demons that I have been fighting.
The only thing keeping me going is writing.
These pages are burning, I've got stories to tell.
Journey's in life that led me through hell.

With life comes troubles and pain that it brings.
I'm like Job in the bible, I've been through some things.
I've seen my way through I've fought many fights.
The storms all around me the lightning it strikes.

Tori Amos told it best, it was me and a gun.
Got the devil on my back, should I lay down or run?
I've been knocked down hard fell flat on the floor.
Screaming out to God "I can't take anymore!"

I've learned that the teacher is quiet during tests.
Learned that people have it worse I should feel I am blessed.
As a child of God I've learned to unpack
All of these burdens I try not to look back.

My faith is strong Lord you know how I feel.
I'm so overwhelmed Jesus please take the wheel.
I only share some of it the rest you can't see.

We all do this sometimes I think you'd agree.

We hide behind questions like how was your day?
I'm hanging in there is what I usually say.
I learned how to swim, jumped from a high dive.
I never gave up, I'm still here, I'm alive.

38. Left Behind

Too busy with social media, we stay up on our phones.
Hypnotizing humanity, we are turning into clones.
They want to give out shots as they line up all the people.
These viruses that they cook up has become very lethal.

They don't want us to think for ourselves, they think that we are blind.
We're being manipulated, dictated to, look at the mess they left behind.
We know they stick together like a bunch of crooked thieves.
The things that they all say, try to make us all believe.

We stay on top of all their news, we all have played along.
But who decides against another, who is right, and who was wrong?
We might vote in these elections, is that supposed to be our voice?
Two or three names on the ballot don't seem like such a choice.

Hard to believe a politician, just watch, just wait, listen.

We watch them debate on who is best, and who will fix our system.
Donors spending money on their words, their poisonous.
We're spitting them back over time, what they have given to us.

While we look down at glass screens, they look at us through our windows.
Things going on behind the scenes, the winds of change it blows.
Things around the world are heating up, there's so much violence.
The future of our kids, they need our love, they need our guidance.

People dying everyday, they don't show us that massacre.
We're all along for the ride, buckle up, you're a passenger.
We look away from many wars, we look away from this genocide.
Flags for coffins on the screens, anyone you recognize?

4. Someone Else

Here comes this vortex again as the world spins on it's axis and I move around all planes of existence. Constant struggles towards that uphill road, knowing when I reach the top, my lost lifestyles will rearrange to become someone else. How many times will I pass through this same hurricane of hope, only to be forced to swirl and slung into someone else's direction? I stand alone sometimes to fill in the holes that someone else has dug. By choice I make decisions while being indecisive and that's just living.

Moving on I stop to enjoy a sunset while others worry that the sunrise will lose it's affect without someone else. So I close my eyes and I'm forced to fly, where dreamsicles are the labyrinth's within the journey. Leading my soul to these inner images where here, I learn to accept reality as a figment of my imagination. Creating my own places within the galaxies of being. So am I real? Or someone else?

39. My Soul To Keep

These demons inside I can't ignore
My body, my mind, my soul is at war.
Atheist, Christian, we can't all be insane
But who is the devil and what is God's name?
We question life, reality, the road ahead
Death, dying, and becoming dead.
I believe in heaven I believe in hell
I believe the devil was an angel who fell.
I believe that Jesus died for our sins
I believe that angel's are sometimes our friends.
I believe what is shown and not what I hear
I believe out of faith and not out of fear.
I believe in God to show me the way
I believe He will do that if I just pray.
He's the only one who's ever stayed
He took my hand when I was afraid.
You might not believe me but I'll tell you how
I came to know Jesus in the here and now.
Wisdom I share from knowledge I grew
You don't know the half of what I been through.
There are some things I can't unsee
Things in life that have changed me.
I've broken mirrors fell off the track
I couldn't go forward without looking back.

There are some lessons I can't unlearn
There are some bridges I can't unburn.
Things in life aren't what they seem
When will we wake up from this dream?
When the horns are drawn and the halos fall?
Is earth a work of art or the luck of the drawl?
Sometimes I fight sometimes I hide
Deep down inside I know I tried.
Philosophical mind that likes to think deep
Who do you pray for your soul to keep?

5. Becoming Dead

Where do you think we all go when we die?
Will we all have wings and know how to fly?
Will it be some place we've been before?
Or new territory we get to explore?
Will we go to this heaven or enter into hell?
I guess we've never been there so how could one tell?
Do you believe in God, where will your soul rest?
A magical nightmare we are put to the test.
How much time do you think it will take to know?
How much of it all do you think God will show?
Do you feel all alone, no one's there for your journey?
Will I see lost loved ones for all of eternity?
Will it all be a dream like some fairy tale?
Will we find out if God is male or female?
Do we have past memories or new things to learn?
I think seeing my dogs is my biggest concern.
Can't wait to get kisses and hug them so tight.
I hope these thoughts turn out to be right.
But what if I'm wrong and stuck in between?
A ghost on earth just waiting to be seen.
A lost soul traveling trying to find a way.
Wondering will this be where I stay?

New Poem

6. Just One

I could tell you stories of things I've been through.
Things you thought you already knew.
My life as told through my perspective.
I leave things out to be protective.
My mind has wondered will it ever be free.
We cannot heal what we do not see.
So I'm pulling off the mask, pulling off the covers.
I'm not the only one there will always be others.
With bipolar disorder and PTSD
 Some live with them both plus anxiety.
Some live with thoughts some call psychotic.
They use words like crazy, insane, neurotic.
Instead of these names for me would you pray?
I speak out for those lost I can show you the way.
I write out these verses my heart is the song.
My faith is my compass has been all along.
No one is perfect we all have sinned.
But I like think that heaven will be in the end.
Highway to hell? I'll go on upstairs.
That's where I'm sending all of my prayers.
For we are not the master of our soul.
God's the Father who's in control.
We all have our beliefs and different views.
Lived different lives, paid different dues.

Some are poor some have much wealth.
Some of us struggle with our mental health.
Some will share stories while others share none.
My name is Traci Martin and I am just one.

40. Mother Earth's College

All of our issues, our problems, they fix em?
Or just set up the world's largest prison system?
While you beg for free health care, medicine and water.
They're fattening us up to die in their slaughter.

Like a pig in a pen you can take down the fence
Been conditioned to stay, like a slave, no defense.
Are you for anti life? What's written on your sign?
Over 70'000 species we murdered over time.

Revenge will be hers we never owned that right
Mother earth out for vengeance she'll put up a fight.
Our plant life now grown in this toxic soil
Demand is high for their synthetic oil.

They pump and pump us full of these lies
Digital dollars track all that we buy.
We're the aliens here not at area 51
You can storm that place smash the mirror when you're done.

Live and die free we're all living on this planet
Straight in the hole is where we all ran it.
We need to fight the alien part in us all

Get back to that earthling in that mirror you saw.

I'd rather live off the land go to mother earth's college
Rather gain in her wisdom than to share their knowledge.
Harm none on your path and I mean Never!
We only have each other got to get through together.

7. End of the Beginning

Laser beam guns at the speed of light.
We alone in the world war fight.
You alone can you sleep at night?
Historical destiny; I dream, I write.

Corporate America with layoffs to share.
Technology has won and nothing is fair.
Now earth is the mother we wear and tear
But beyond this place our soul is rare.

Asleep in your bed they learn who you are.
Material mass and dust of star.
For someone who shut a porthole left ajar
I stayed in too long and went in too far.

Into a realm designed in space.
Welcome you all to the human race.
Goodbye to your mind they wish to erase
We're sheltered by God who knows of this place.

Scattered noises gathered day by day.
Where will you be in a moment away?
Their video game World War 3 to play
As we ask the controllers to stop and pray.

My dream is eternal as the sky is blue.
Wisdom I share from knowledge I grew.
From talks with God I envisioned it through.
So I write it all down to share it with you.

Reading my words while asking for more.
Pages I've wrote on upcoming war.
While demons await to settle a score
Fallen angel my time has come to soar.

A moment in time a life at least.
Alone I have traveled to defeat this beast.
Asking for strength and my inner peace.
Knowing war for your soul will never cease.

Upside down my world's been bent.
Words of wisdom I knew God lent.
From a path above it's life he sent.
And this end to a beginning of death well spent.

41. Spiritual Orphan

A spiritual orphan with prophetic visions she dreams in black and white.
She runs through all these dark tunnels at the end there might be light.
She was like Eve in a garden of evil tempted by these things.
Wanting to know the secrets to life, what knowledge that it brings.

Questioning God on why he allows bad things to happen here.
The world as we know it is broken and we broke it out of fear.
The devil will try to tempt her, turn us all into his tenants.
He's looking for those lost and broken, falling angels, his descendants.

She sings these ancient hymns at night like the harmonies of birds.
She painted her skin in memories, her soul's made out of words.
She's given this body but only for a moment until it is replaced.

Her souls a vessel to travel through all time and all of space.

Where wicked spirits are in these realms, these demons she has been shown.
She likes to wander around here freely, she often travels alone.
She's multiplying infinity and dividing up her days.
While she was walking through this forest she ended up inside this maze.

8. Wish I would have knew

He's been working on my story since the day that I was born.
I write my words in ink and the page is my platform.
I try to share my stories with others, things I've ever felt.
Some they've had it worse than the cards that I've been dealt.

I've been down may rabbit holes there's some things that I can tell.
I've never been to heaven I've taken many trips through hell.
I've lived through many moments, felt the passing of time through minutes.
I've loved, I've lost, I've started all over, been pushed to my outer limits.

He takes the good, he takes the bad, and uses them for growth.
He found me hanging near the bottom, tied a knot at the end of my rope.
He said "Hang on tight ,there's always hope, help is on the way.
I will come meet you right where you are, just talk to me when you pray."

While I was standing still just listening God was picking teams.
He used my tears to water seeds, implanted were my dreams.
Not found on any GPS, look inside for peace, you'll find it.
Sometimes you have to go off grid and sit where it's real quiet.

If patience teaches you anything it's sometimes you have to wait.
If reality is what you make of it your thoughts are what you create.
Time will pass and time will tell and life is not a race.
What I find when I am by myself, I enjoy all of my space.

Some believe in many truths, I find to be what's real
Depends on where you come from and how it makes you feel.
We all have lost our cool out of anger and frustration.
We've all been judged by others, we've faced discrimination.

Words can be used as weapons, so what will you choose to write?
Will it be about all those dark days, or when you finally

seen the light?
I've lived, I've learned, I'm not going back to the things that I was shown.
I've put the pieces back together I pray when I'm alone.

Everything I've done and all the things I've ever been through
There in my past, I'm not looking back, just wish I would have knew.

42. Open Book

I wanted to write some things down, to write them as I see.
That's the way my brain is wired, inside my circuitry.
I share so many things that are deep down in my soul.
About how life has taken turns and also took it's toll.
I've learned some lessons hard ways, we all have went that way.
Stories that are hard to tell that no one else would say.
I held my breath so long one time I wanted to pass out.
No question I was manic, took an exit off my route.
I seen some things others did not, I've lived through this facade.
I threw out all my things to be closer to my God.
I stopped and listened quietly, I heard it through the birds.
A suitcase with my books inside, I kept all of my words.
Some journals and some poetry, my testimony speaks.
An open book you will find the answers that you seek.

9. The Natural Realm

There's never been a successful civilization in the natural realm
They all bring war, disease and death, we've captured that on film.
We've turned down natural law and science for opinions and theories
We're distracted by political parties and your next netflix series.

As their adding their amendments the constitutions being arranged
Just another set of rules and regulations that they changed.
We're being controlled, we're being conditioned, brainwashed by all the media.
They are giving you your opinions why you take what they are feeding ya.

Some grazing at the trough of entertainment like their cattle.
With broken backs, broken dreams, a broken system we all battle.
Untying all the knots before we die from being strangled.

Their spinning webs of deception let's start to get untangled.

Their advertising to us to keep us hidden from things we missed.
Facts don't change because the media told us to do this.
When you politicize something like opinions it's only argued about
No action is taken, you only question and start to truly doubt.

The politicians? The elite? Or a mix of these snake charmers.
We were born into this system, a human farm, who are the farmers?
We are livestock to the masters and we graze on what they feed.
An experimental playground they don't expect us to stampede.

They poison our food, our water, our minds, don't say you were not warned.
They want to kill the criminal before the criminal has been born.
This class warfare they use on us will make us all the targets.
If we the people make up the system then we control the

markets.

Some are pawns in this matrix, missing pieces of the puzzle.
Now the tyrants are the healthy who won't wear their face muzzle.
Land of the free, home of the slave as they take what's mine and yours.
Truth becoming propaganda while they profit off these wars.

43. The Mazzstarr Of The Universe
For my daughter Mazzy Starr

She likes to sing, she likes to dance, she likes to be a kid.
But she's taken more than I'll ever know, more than what has been said.
This child has dealt with loss in life and overcame some storms.
She's learning to cope, to deal with life and all it's many forms.
I want to soothe her soul for her inner child's unique.
The ways of the world are very cruel, inside she sought to seek.
She writes in pages then rips them out, her trust has been affected.
She paints these pictures in her mind when she feels she's been rejected.
People will gossip and people will judge, some kids aren't very nice.
Keep your head above it all, I offer my best advice.
I'll be by your side, good or bad, I'll always be around.
You can tell me anything and I'll tell you what I have

found.
Do what is right inside your heart you know what I have shown.
Be yourself even if this means you have to stand alone.

10 . Systems Down Rant

Lost in a swirl of a chaotic blend
Mixing my enemies amongst my friends
Once I learn their rules and then I will send
For you can keep but I know I will bend
All of these games they try to amend
While you believe they play pretend
Only in the end to me they offend.

Why do we let this system prevail?
For all of us are subject to fail
They hunt the streets and waters we sail
For their opinions we are hauled off to jail
Only to them to collect our bail
While going home to more bills in the mail.

Where is all the money they collect?
For when in pain they eagerly accept
To take their help is to regret
In the end they never forget.
To the mansions they live we pay the rent
Taking chunks out my paycheck has left a dent
And all I can do is Vent! Vent! Vent!
While I go home to my tent
And look at mail that is sent

And my money that is meant
Not for me they have spent
On my mind that has went.

44. Sir Maxwell The Fuzzy 10-10-05~ 12-10-18

Sir Maxwell the fuzzy he was my baby boy
Brought love in this world he was my pride and joy.
We had this connection in his eyes I would stare
No other fur baby could ever compare.
The best dog in the world, I know, I have seen
Played with toys like a puppy till age thirteen.
He had this obsession with licking your feet
Rocked a blue mohawk everyone thought was neat.
People took pictures wherever we went
I know that for me he was heaven sent.
I could let him off leash he would always come back
I rewarded with treats he would wait for his snack.
This boy was my shadow, by my side he was found
He would do this trick where he spun all around.
When I had a bad day he would sense something was wrong
He'd lay down beside me and it wouldn't take long.
He melted my heart took all worries away
I just wished he lived longer but he couldn't stay.
He was in much pain and this was just his time
Held him in my arms; told him he'd be fine.
Over the rainbow bridge I will see him again.
Truly one of a kind, he was my best friend.

11. Inner Stand

If you ever called me friend and you showed up by my side.
If you ever in those moments stood with me when people died.
If you ever held my hand, wiped my tears, felt my pain.
If you've ever been in chapters of my life when I'm not sane.
The ones that take the time are the ones who truly try.
The ones that read me word for word while others pass me by.
I've known some of you only years and some I've known since birth.
They say that blood is thicker than water but water makes up the earth.
If you knew me as your family and tell stories of the past.
If you knew me through my childhood then you know I grew up fast.
I've played in dirt, I've climbed some trees, played baseball with the boys.
Now that I'm much older just want quiet from all the noise.
If you really looked inside me, through the eyes and through the soul.

You took a journey not many have right down that rabbit hole.
To really inner stand me, who I am and love because.
The person that I am now, not the person I once was.

45. Happy Father's Day poem to my dad Marty Martin who passed away March 3, 2025

Happy father's day to the man I've known since birth.
Marty Martin, my dad, who taught me what I'm really worth.
When I was just a little girl we jammed music in his truck.
We listened to XL102 when the music didn't suck.
Dad asked one day why I listen to "Noise", heavy metal, I let him know
I was 5 years old, in his truck, when Ironman came on the radio.
I told him it's all Ozzy's fault but I still love rock and roll.
I love all kinds of music, anything that moves my soul.
We lived out in the country, that's where I was born and raised.
Dukes of Hazzard on the TV and all the messes that we made.
Growing up in the 80's we didn't need any babysitters.
Dad called me Ellie Mae cause I take care of all the critters.

I was watching horror movies so young, Exorcist was the first.
At 6 years old, saw that head spin around, I thought I would be cursed.
Dad had these scary masks he'd scare us with late at night.
I'd have friends over, he'd knock on the window, and give us all a fright.
Mom told me about a ZZ Top concert and dad's top hat.
He went to get a beer, fell down all the steps, and he went splat!
When I was little dad woke me up, to sing, he'd play his guitar.
I'd sing for him Janis Joplin, my favorite, I was his star.
I was always daddy's girl, those memories I hold them close.
I miss his sense of humor and all his funny jokes.
He'd say "I don't have everything I want but I have everything I need"
All dad really wanted was to win the lottery and smoke his weed.
He sat on the porch everyday and "Watched the world go by."
Things will never be the same since the day my daddy died.
I lived with dad, we took care of each other, he was my very best friend.

It was hard to say good bye, when my road ends we'll meet again...

12. Lighthouse

This new way of life is what they want you to be
A political land of illusion you see.
I am not a label, I don't follow the right
I don't follow the left I just use my eyesight.

Their open air prison don't want nowhere near it.
I'm on this battlefield with my fighting spirit.
We were not designed to live like this.
We need to rise, rebel, and then resist.

United we live divided we die
We will be the new slaves if we don't even try.
Nothing left for our kids we're destroying this planet.
Fake news? Fact check: They don't like it they ban it.

They use social media to see how we feel.
Realist pay attention because we know the deal.
We gave them the power to feed all of us.
It gave them power to starve now who do you trust?

Selling out our country with our money in their hand.
Eminent domain now their stealing our land.
Free speech now censored by these communist.
Don't bring up the past, tear down monuments.

Their dividing us now, we all struggle, armed strife.
Diversity is our strength it's our way of life.
They use fear on us and group mentality.
Social media becoming our new reality.

A new way of socializing without catching germs.
Wear your mask, wash your hands, abide by their terms.
While cashing in on their profits we're out on a limb.
They made it too toxic to live without them.

We follow them blindly not reading the signs.
They poisoned our waters, they poisoned our minds.
The USA belongs to we the people.
Our land is our strength, our future, our prequel.

Don't believe their lies their errors are provable
We must become like the lighthouse, unshakable,
unmovable.

52.

13. New World Disorder

I've listen very patiently while others speak their truth.
I've googled things, read many books, searched government sites for proof.
Everyone doing their own research, tell me what website you entered.
Time to question the words being used and why we're all being censored.

No privacy settings, we're all exposed, social media access granted.
News becoming weaponized as ideas are being implanted.
A fake blanket of securities, just wear your mask and wash your hands.
Keep your distance, stay apart, six feet away everyone stands.

1% of the population putting mandates on us, the majority.
This new world order has tyrants acting like they have all the authority.
Keep us guessing what comes next, what tricks are up their sleeves.
What's right or wrong, where to find truth, fresh fruit

from knowledge trees.

We've all experienced economic struggles while dealing with this virus.
But there's a blueprint for our bodies with an immune system inside us.
I keep planting all these seeds, I find the light, I grow, project it.
Talk to God when I'm feeling down, feeling lost, and being rejected.

I use my words to translate things from a global observation.
A poetic earth child warrior I begin this manifestation.
I claim individual sovereignty, authority over myself.
No need for government dictators to tell me what I felt.

These evil rulers in the heavenly realms need a serious intervention.
This sacred arithmetic of time tells of spiritual redemption.
There are demons speaking through human mouths, we need to break the chains.
This spiritual war we're fighting in through history has left bloodstains.

We never question why these wars were fought in the

first place.
Invading countries for resources while leaving them nuclear waste.
All seeing all the things we do in everything He knows.
God gave me my first breath and only He knows how this goes.

46. Canvas In The Sky

My thoughts outnumber the grains of sand in time they'll be translated.
I was given a gift, these choice of words, like a prophet he created.
Something inside me knows something bigger than I exist.
This intelligent design was by someone creating this.

If I study chemistry and physics, the law of the land.
There's a digital code inside my cells almost like it was planned.
If science and my faith point to this reality.
I will battle good and evil, struggle with duality.

I'm at an intersection of hope, I am living on the edge.
A rock in a hard place is where I'm at, it's where I'm wedged.
I ask a complex question "Is this life an accident?"
Or some divine design, some deliberate intent?

I know there's purpose to my life, some roles I must fulfill.
I'm a mother with a daughter with characteristics to instill.

Like how to help the homeless, give them something they can eat.
Help those with mental health issues, when lost they feel defeat.

I want her to know I love her, just how beautiful she is
She's the reason why I keep going, the reason why I live.
She should also know those insecurities will disappear one day.
She'll realize why they never mattered and why God has made her that way.

I'm also a daughter, I try to help, I love my mom and dad.
I know they did the best they could with what all that we had.
Childhood was not an easy thing for me it had rough spots.
But it taught me how to hold on tight, be humble and what not.

I'm also a sister, an Irish twin, to a brother that I love.
We've walked through hell together, found out what we're made up of.
We went through some hard times, things got bad, it was tough.
There were times we didn't speak, I hated him, I'd had enough.

Now we have each other's backs, forgiveness goes both ways.
Sometimes I shed a tear when I think back to all those days.
I'm also a spoken word poet, I try to write all of this down.
The things I've seen, times spent lost, how I felt when I was found.

If God made me to love me than I'll place no one above
The cosmological constant, the Devine Design is Love.
I have faith and I have hope, I'll have some proof before I die.
When He paints my story where it belongs, my canvas in His sky.

14. New Woke Order

The world as we know it has disappeared when will we intervene?
This artificial intelligence they created the machine.
The system was designed to crash, they make out in the end.
But some of you act like these politicians are your friend.

They use tactics like the soviets to make us want to kill each other.
Now this social distancing got us fearing our own brother.
They fear those with the knowledge and control those without it.
The same people who sell the panic, sell the pill, just take a bit.

They're organizing medicine, we've been taking what they give.
Why do I care about dying if I'm denied the right to live?
All your rights you thought you had they've written them as wrong.
The time for this has been coming they knew it all along.

False prophets in sheep's clothing you'll know them by

their fruits.
Their carbon footprints planted deep, I'm chopping at their roots.
The timing of these tidal waves through this storm they will surge.
If you take away police, we kill each other in this purge.

This social theatre you all act in take a look at your own reflections.
If the system leaves us high and dry who would be your connections?
I've felt the flames of hell so many demons I did meet.
I have these battle scars, I have suffered past defeat.

A real warrior doesn't want to battle, he does not want a war.
He knows he has his weaknesses and what his strengths are for.
The savior that's inside of me, I question him, I do.
All knowing and all seeing all the things that we go through.

I've encountered Him through many storms his grace I did receive.
My trust, my faith, my confidence, in God I do believe.
For what we seek we already have, true power comes from within.

And once you do believe the signs are everywhere you've been.

So make your existence a legend, or even remembered at all.
For what goes up must come down, true freedom they outlaw.
We use flags and borders to divide us, technologies made us blind.
Connect the dots for the bigger picture or you'll get left behind.

15. The Looking Glass

Truth is just a concept, just a word that we should question.
Survival of the fittest means natural selection.
So many things have happened over time let cultures speak.
Take care of all our elders they have the knowledge that we seek.
The present moment is happening now it wasn't designed to last.
We move forward in the future but we can't forget our past.
We're all born at different moments in time, my parents born in the 50"s.
Make love not war a slogan used for peace during the 60"s.
I was born in 77, made it through up until now.
Been through some things that made me think of throwing in the towel.
Growing up the the 1980's, just a kid viewing the world.
Like a caterpillar to a butterfly, my imagination did swirl.
In the 1990"s I graduated, went on tour with the Grateful Dead.
Experienced life, the freedom to be all the peaceful things I read.

On September 11th 2001 the terrorist attacks occurred.
I thought it was the end of the world, I truly felt disturbed.
If we're unable to stand up to tyranny, One nation under God will fall.
If we're unable to control our emotions, we can't control anything at all.
We're giving up freedoms for safety; Code Red we are in danger!
I feel like I'm in the twilight zone and it's only getting stranger.
The world's become dark, cold and brutal, it's left some of you heartless.
We need some light inside of this world, lead our own way out of darkness.
Lead us not into temptation but deliver us from evil.
Deliver us from tyrants trying to kill us and make it legal.
Our reflections of who we used to be are written in the past.
Mirror images of ourselves, we are one in the looking glass.

16. Visual of Identity

Who lived before time itself, who made it through the flood?
The search for immortality, our DNA, what's in our blood.
Many years ago from here, far off into the distance
A sequence of code, we're made up of began our very existence.

Before there was a single molecule, before there was this atom
After God became lonely, he created angels to have them.
To the Anunnaki from the heavens and then they came to earth.
To Adam and Eve, who bit the apple, and who would give the birth.

We've had prehistoric contact with some prehistoric skulls.
Wicked spirits in the heavenly realms, and fallen are the angels.
We all know the creation story, on the 7th day he rest.
We are all just visitors here, are we the extraterrestrial guest?

If heaven is up and hell is down and earth is in between
Then there has to be angels and demons and other things we have not seen.
The great unknown we speak about, I learned don't sink, I swam.
This divine intelligence from within, from God, The Great I Am.

Made are we in his image, and things people will see.
Our origin of species, our visual of identity.
Where did our soul come from, where has it been before?
These questions all have answers, how far will you explore?

We question why there are certain things that He has deemed forbidden.
Will we ever know the answers to life or will He keep them hidden?
We all have fears and questions, what's this life really about?
We all go through trials and tribulations and a shadow of a doubt.

We are born into this world and we all die all alone.
Everyone's walk is different and the things that we are

shown.
I once was blind but now I see, was lost but now I'm found.
A tattoo on my wrist with music notes wrapped all around.

We live in the present, we have a future, we lived through all of the past.
People die every day our bodies weren't built to last.
No one knows the day or how much time they have to live.
How many times we failed him and he still chose to forgive.

I've learned to pray and thank Him, even for the really tough times.
It's all about perspective and how to read all of the signs.
Some will never believe even when you show them proof.
I guess in the end all of us will find out what's the truth.

17. Digital Genesis

The webs become a cult, what's your dependency on it?
We share things in our feeds, on our pages we see fit.
We use our judgement, our influence, over people we try to change.
Sometimes we pay the price for trying to do all the right things.

We spend our time in speculation, not enough of certainty.
They divide us with misinformation, make us question our identity.
For alone we feel oppressed, like we're the only ones who suffer.
They want to keep us separated, for our power comes in numbers.

They might have the upper hand right now, for wealth is their advantage.
But we've been learning to live with less, there's no way they'd ever manage.
To live without us means losing our labor, their money would have no value.
Tribalistically we'd have to look out for each other, for our children we'd do what we had to.

Why they request a new world order, they project on us blue beams.
Their mind control of the masses as we stare down at glass screens.
The mind of the consciousness, goes to war, it starts debating.
The cerebral cortex starts a beat, it starts this inward pulsating.

The artist drawing lines in the sky will block out all of the sun.
The shepherd in the heavens will cancel him, and he'll be done.
They keep pushing their agendas, they keep pushing all the buttons.
For crimes against humanity we're exposing all of the gluttons.

If you want to change the outcome then speak up, and hold your sign.
For the change you seek, it starts with you, one conversation at a time.
We need to put aside our differences, like our race, and our religions.
It's all up to we the people, the 99% of all the citizens.

Society is a team sport, no matter the lives that we were dealt.
This govern mint has gotten to big and it's not going to reform itself.
Who came up with the left or right? Same bird just different feather.
If we're all pieces to a puzzle then who puts it all together?

In the beginning the word was God, now we write in our own sentences.
As we start to ask the real questions in this digital genesis.

18. A Day Away From The World

Just in time for a little sunrise on the tips of cloud nine as I awaken on my day away from the world. I'm standing up on the inside for my spirit walks alone in this body. Will I plan to stay awhile as time multiplies infinity and divides the days into the final production of his script? We all remember Genesis being in the beginning so where did we lose each other in the past? And will we all join in the future?

See, the moon is my compass in darkness awakening this creator of creativity. Maybe I'm philosophical but I'm still writing. It is my day away from the world. Who knows? My words may maneuver there way into your path and if they do and you hear me and you understand: You might be blessed with a day away from the world.

This gravitational pull will project a trail ahead. Above the clouds below the earth lies infinity. I'm flying free with the birds and the bees while soaring through these snowstorms with colored faeries. Floating free on the waters of my islands. Surfing the rain in his storms I dream. And I awake from my day away from the world. Swallowing the drama of the outside world I stomach the pain while indulged in silence. Indulged in thoughts which are only mine. Indulged in the sunrise and the beauty of all things. So is the world a day away from me?

19. Built Different

You ever think about Helen Keller who couldn't see or hear?
At 19 months she lost her sight and hearing, showed no fear.
She became an American author, an advocate for disability rights.
A political activist and lecturer I'd say she knew how to fight.

She used her fingers to spell words, self taught communication.
If one became blind and couldn't see, they'd use this information.
Some times we have these obstacles that always get in the way.
Like a tree who's roots are planted deep, I'll bear fruit if I just stay.

He placed me next to a river, it's currents pulled me in.
I was no match for all the temptations, we give in to all these sins.
The power of the flesh, an obstacle for your soul spirit.
You have to learn to use your head but the hearts the one who steers it.

Your birth ship is your vessel, built and formed inside your mother.
Like paper boats designed by God then gifted to one another.
When the winds just right, the timing set, he breathes life into our sails.
He sets in motion a journey, a path, we all have told our tales.

Sometimes the water gets polluted, the kind you don't swim in.
You can hang on to the dolphins but the sharks they ain't your friend.
We've all swam in shallow waters, but some of us explore the deep.
When it comes to faith, belief in Him, sometimes you have to leap.

A mustard seed is very small, some planted some are thrown.
What happens to them both the world is filled with the unknown.
Endless possibilities, calculations, add and subtract.
The value of two mathematical expressions are equal and that's a fact.

20. ; Semi-Colon ;

Many times I've gotten back up from all the times I fell.
Close to the broken hearted he saves those lost and stuck in hell.
We all fall short to the glory of him no ten commandments kept.
We testify to what we have seen and some will not accept.

I was in a bad place when I lost myself he came and gave a nudge.
He told me some would not understand those people they will judge.
PTSD, bi polar, depression, anxiety I have been through.
I share my story to those that know my story could have been you.

At 23 bad people I met, Fayettnom North Carolina drug dealers.
Chanting spells way up in trees encountered these witch healers.
Soldiers going AWOL through this cult like thing I found.
Many different people, many faces all around.

I wrote these poems from things I heard, they thought I knew too much.
Bad things they did, bad cops they knew, and so the story is such.
My brother came to get me, tried to find me just in time.
Carried me out before my death, all my things I left behind.

I found this God I know inside, this voice I start to hear it.
I walked through hell to get to him, my guide the holy spirit.
I've contemplated suicide way back: that is in the past.
My storms they come and go but were never meant to last.

I tell my story to get it out and maybe just to show.
We all have different stories, unique, and people that we know.

21. Coexist

This land is your land this land is my land... Is this land really free?
Our threat levels high, we're on high alert, to things that we don't see.
No freedom of rights they are taken away, these laws of rejection.
Is he president or infidel, just what is the connection?

Does anyone know who's running this ship, who's really operating?
We the people will disagree while politicians keep debating.
Divide and conquer is their plan, we all play in this game.
They keep us pointing fingers at each other who's to blame?

We jump from one thing to another let's just agree to disagree.
We fight through all our differences we deal with controversy.
It's not just racism we're trying to beat, we all are under attack.
We all have social media friends but who's really got

your back?

Someone will always comment just to prove that they are right.
Together we stand for equality but some just like to fight.
They keep us separated for a reason from the truth.
Not everything is all fake news some of us have our proof.

Some watch tv to get their news while others pray and think.
We all are in the same boat together but who is making it sink?
It's not the politicians or the system we can trust.
This new normal they talk about it comes from all of us.

No one is sure of what comes next, in our minds we will conceive.
We've all been cruising on auto pilot being shown what to believe.
I believe that money is the root to all evil, not just a fairytale.
You can follow their recommendations, I'll follow the money trail.

You can stay in fear of what they say or protest in the streets.
Some of us are waking up while others are fast asleep.
We all have our own belief system from things in life we learned.
The things that I have seen that you have not, I'd start to be concerned.

We don't need to go back to how things were but some they will relapse.
While you be the shepherd or be the sheep when this whole thing does collapse?
The stores opened during quarantine all have their empty shelves.
We need to find what matters most, get back inside ourselves.

They treat us like we're lab rats being tested so many ways.
We're all just trying to survive to get through the next phase.
We need to show compassion and forgiveness of each other.
No matter the color of your skin you're my sister, you are my brother.

My sin is white and this has put me on a separate list.

White privilege a term that's throw around we all try to resist.
While some were born into this hate I'm against all bigotry.
If we could live life as if we were one then we would really be free.

But the government controls the opposition we pay cause we've been bought.
Tongue of torture all around this racism has been taught.
Hate groups still around do you see them now? It's hard to ignore.
News of different races, different people waging war.

We are fighting with each other but who's taking and who's giving?
This indoctrinated hate their keeping life from all the living.
Our eyes can distinguish black from white we make our own decisions.
From channel to channel we watch what they put on our televisions.

History shows that some were forced, to be slaves based on their race.
Taken from their homelands, bought and sold and put in this place.

They've dealt with groups of white supremacy like the KKK.
Hate for blacks and jews and anyone who might be gay.

They were chased down, they were hung in trees, hung them by a noose.
If history repeats itself we're exposing all these truths.
No longer these groups are hiding, they are here and everywhere.
Starting race wars in our hometowns, Antifa we are aware.

These white supremacist turned terrorist their scared of the majority.
White nationalist they call them in the news now their the threatened minority.
Their tearing stuff up, their burning our buildings, and taking some of our lives.
Waving their flags of hatred while giving each other high fives.

Freedom of speech they spew their hate but with a bulletproof vest.
Our president of the united states must surely be impressed.
I blame some of our leaders for the wars we will have to fight.

Remember to vote in November and put a stop to the alt right.

If we the people could speak out on the things that we believe.
Stop taking on the mindset of the media who deceives.
They use the first amendment to protect their freedom of speech.
I choose to change the channel, it's my pastor I watch preach.

We've watched nation against nation, we've watched man against man.
I've watched revelation in the bible play out as if God's plan.
Differences aside we're all children of God's descendants.
Democrats, republicans, liberals and independents.

They use these smoking mirrors to distract us from the truth.
Keep us fighting one another with fake news that has no proof.
People telling stories of the past that they were taught.
We all were sold some lies, they were paid and we were bought.

Some believe that the elite with their money they

control.
Everything about us we're being stripped down to our soul.
The battle between good and evil, we fight for what we need.
They control our source of food, who you think they'll choose to feed?

We've woken up the world on injustice and corruption.
But if we don't stop with all the hate, it'll lead to our destruction.
Black or white I think we can agree some have more privilege.
But if we're going to beat the system it's going to take a village.

No need for all the violence or breaking all the laws.
All of us together fighting for each others cause.
The times they are a changing but we know time goes by fast.
We don't know what the future holds but we can't repeat the past.

We all just want to understand where each of us have been.
I have a daughter to protect, we have family, we have friends.

I don't have all the answers, I'm sure there's things I missed.
But one thing that I know for sure we have to coexist.

22. Divided States Of America

Divided states of America we all will fall.
Brother's getting shot, did they brake the law?
National anthems, who stood and who sat?
Telling our kids what we think about that.

American Indians gather for a peaceful protest.
This land is who's land when they start to arrest?
They take away land and contaminate water.
Don't want your pipeline that's not a good barter.

People standing up for what they believe.
Tear gas in their eyes they start to receive.
They want you to believe what's on your TV.
Picking and choosing the things you will see.

It must be true if you seen it on Facebook.
Fact checking through google we all take a look.
Cell phone zombies they got us sedated.
When you keep looking down the world becomes faded.

The facts are never in before they give us these clues.
But we keep on believing what we hear in the news.
We're lost in this world where racisms found.

What do you see when you look around?

Economy's down we're down on our luck.
Into a trap, we're caught, we're stuck.
While a hungry child searches we stifle the cries.
Luring us in with intoxicating lies.

These scholars of war infusing the hate.
They open the borders and then lock the gate.
We're divided by people, divided our nation.
A prophetic dream, annihilation.

This highway to hell has been paved.
Apocalyptic world for the un saved.
Bloodless donor all dried up.
Glass half full or empty cup?

We're living beings under microscopes.
Hidden silence, suicide ropes.
Naked secrets, body aches.
Mother nature's earth that quakes.

A generation destroyed by madness.
Death of our people and so much sadness.
Democrat, republican, who's the most patriotic?
Insane, deranged, demented, psychotic.

So many wars and conflicts debated.
Heated discussions we walk away hated.
The right to bear arms and then give it to children.
Detonating your bombs just what are you building?

Made in China bought and sold.
Silver diamonds made of gold.
Walkie talkies replaced by phones
GPS and arial drones.

Freedoms not free if you have to defend her.
Remember to forget, to relent, to surrender.
Collateral damage on parallel lines.
Are we living in the end of times?

Home of the brave and the ones who have fought.
Who's land of the free, have we all been bought?

23. Becoming Me

Like a caterpillar to a butterfly I've been going through these changes.
It's like learning to fly without wings, the process not so painless.
It's like drowning underwater, try to breathe, I'm out of breath.
It's like walking through the valley of the shadow of my death.
All those times I almost gave up, wishing I had died.
I've smiled at times, you'd never know, what I have tucked inside.
I feel I have the largest part of hell inside of me.
I battle depression like a war on terror, it's hard sometimes to see.
It takes all that I got, to remain calm inside this storm.
I've been riding these tidal waves since the day that I was born.
It's like one thing after another and it's piling up so fast.
These burdens putting pressure on me I feel I might not last.
By faith I shouldn't worry or have all of these fears.
But every time I take the wheel the devil switches gears.
The past becomes the past I try to leave it all behind.
Unknown is the future, don't know who or what I'll find.

24. Me, Myself And I

I've looked for myself, I've stared into mirrors.
We've been together for forty eight years.
We've walked through life, broken pieces of heart.
Felt love then hate as we were torn apart.
Taught that society would always judge.
The size of our waist while we hold a grudge.
We cannot believe what we have become.
Hard on ourselves it's so easy for some.
Had to learn that with life there's love and suffering.
Pain in my mind I know we're still recovering.
Went through many test of our patience and will.
We've held it together cause we know the drill.
I hate to admit, don't know much about you.
I can only tell stories of the things I've been through.

25. One Of A Kind

One voice, one vision, I'm one of a kind.
Get lost in the mix and get left behind.
They play these games and then press rewind.
Trust is an issue we're forced to find.

A realm seeker by dreams, my nightly reality.
When gateways were opened to this locality.
When you live in a world with this mentality'
Innocence is lost in doomed fatalities.

Visions of life pass through a porthole.
Robbing experience with hearts it stole.
From times I have spent with you as my goal.
Rocking in chairs, your hand to my soul.

To the one that you pick to a stupid mistake.
Who will you choose for the love that you make?
I'll travel your way but it's my path I take.
Emotions run high when relationships break.

Souring spirit a journey, my heart to free.
One of a kind is a hard thing to be.
Letting them in as they learn to see me.

But who will I meet and will they agree?
I'm one of a kind.

26. The Crush

Nervous as hell to tell you how I feel, I've only got one shot.
I picked up the pen and put it to paper and this is what I got.
Truth drips on the page where you entered I want to plant this seed.
I pull at this arrow in my heart my thoughts they start to bleed.
You're like some kind of magic, you've cast some kind of spell.
I spun the bottle, it landed on you, and head over heels I fell.
Something you have is very real but it could just be a thought.
You catch my eye when you walk by my attention is now caught.
I feel you belong to no one, you wander around here freely.
Magnetic you are like a piece of my soul, I let you in to see me.
I'm intently present on these unspoken words I write for you to find.
As you slide into my visions, I tip toe through your mind.

Everything must be arranged by the tempo of the dance.
I took my time to write this rhyme then leave it up to chance.
Wondering your thoughts inside my thoughts, inside my mind they grew.
You turn it up and then you go, I'm left without a clue.
I want to venture into your world as I seek you run and hide.
I want to show you how I feel I want to let you inside.
This scene in my head, I write it down, but not sure how it ends.
This ache in my heart, I feel it now, for you it does begin.
Like a breathing canvas you make the strokes as I hold onto the brush.
I paint the picture perfect for you then titled it the crush.

27. Potion Of A Pimpstress

A field of cupids await us all.
Pick and choose as the arrows fall.
Your presence I command to wander in.
Unchartered dreams I play to win.
Potion of a pimp is my state of mind.
Soul mates I've had left me behind.
New love an intensity that leaves you lost.
Magnetic your force my heart the cost.
A melodic melody these butterflies pound.
You tangle my wings when you come around.
Charmed by your spirit I enter a trance.
Mysterious creatures escape to dance.
Hypnotize your eyes to flirt with desire.
Discover my journeys to take you higher.
Inhale my emotions I never waste.
Exhale through your mind this tempting place.
Let me dominate time while you take my hand.
Enter me now upon fantasy land.
While I dance with fate and fly with faeries.
An earthbound Goddess it's you that carries.
The divine instructions of riding the wind.
Curiosity is fed as we play pretend.
Poetically what I write is real.
Mystical creation with sex appeal.

If you like what you hear than express it to me.
My ears are open my mind is free.
My soul is searching it's you I see.
For all others have failed and now you hold the key.

28. Drive The Test Of Time

Two different souls
Two different paths
I travel the roads less taken
You frequent the highways I've passed.

So allow me to show you a detour
A journey through my eyes
For two souls to become one
Is a road without lies.

Trust in me and I'll trust in you
To build new roads with love
There are some highways left unfinished
And some roads we go alone.

The ride we take may be bumpy
Maybe have a curve or two
But if we stick together
The steerings up to me and you.

So handle your soul well
I'll have a check up on mine
We'll put the two together
And drive the test of time.

29. Keeper Of My Heart

If you could see into the future would you take a look inside?
One minute your in the present moment then you leave the past behind.
It's like choose your own adventure where each chapter is your choice.
Your instincts help to lead the way as you learn that inner voice.

I've walked some miles, I never gave up, it made it worth the wait.
That fallen star I wished upon it must have brought me fate.
I looked to the sky, while counting stars , those planets did align.
I looked into your eyes and found myself inside of time.

The way we fit together like puzzle pieces and melody's.
The man of my dreams, you came into my life, and changed reality.
You are my strength when I am weak, there is magic in your touch.
The warmth of your skin, your kiss on my lips, I love them oh so much.

I love to be within your arms, your hugs they get me by.
I love your voice, your energy, that sparkle in your eye.
I love the way you hold me close, I long for that embrace.
I love the way you look at me, I see it in your face.

I could go on forever, if you'd like I'd tell you more.
But I like to keep a little mystery, I like when we explore.
I like that there are some things that are yet to be discovered.
In time all of these questions you have will start to be uncovered.

I waited my whole life for you a new chapter we will start.
A beautiful mind inside an old soul, you are the keeper of my heart.

30. The Lyrics To My Heart

Further down the river is where I found you.
I want to know things that you are into.
Everything I learn I want to know more.
No games to be played your love is the score.
On the wings of maybe I feel for your heart.
Unsure of the outcome, unsure where to start.
Let's embark on a journey just look in my eyes.
Look into my soul that's where the truth lies.
The words that I write are as they appear.
I want you to listen, I want you to hear.
Patiently I've stood here on you I have waited.
Got my mind in a trance and my body's sedated.
I'm dreaming in visions I see them all through.
At the end of this dream I want to see you.
I knew there was something there so I tried.
You drew love from my veins when I let you inside.
Into some feelings I might have just fell.
The scent that you left behind I still smell.
My sense of direction is pointing to you.
Time travels in waves I see my way through.
Counterclockwise it never ends it seems.
Like I'm spinning on my axis, you rotate in my dreams.
In your world I seek will you play or hide?
Trust how you feel if you just let me inside.

Two of a kind who's hearts have been broken.
Between you and me this language is spoken.
I want to know things that you never say.
The things that are thought when I am away.
I know what's inside I know what I feel.
I want to know you is this love for real?
Every once in awhile you can give me a sign.
Still be yourself I just want to spend time.
I want to sit and stare right through.
Wondering your thoughts in my mind they grew.
I'd tear down my walls if you'd stay awhile.
I've never met anyone with your unique style.
Love these feelings inside that you bring
Love the music you send me for you I would sing.
When the stars align I hope you'll be my guide.
Our souls dance like the moon when it pulls at the tide.
I'm under the influence the influence of you.
What sober couldn't say sober couldn't do.
My heart is guarded it's your kind I feared.
When I wished for love and then you appeared.
My chest is pounding my heart skips a beat.
I will not let our past become our defeat.
Lying in my vessel my heart overflows.
These feelings inside I want you to know.
Kindred spirits no need to pretend.
No need for rules we have to bend.
I'm into you it's you I'm digging.

Time stands still but time is still ticking.
Cupid will shoot his arrows will fall.
Into your court I drop the ball.
What I want most is more than just friends.
Shy like you I don't know how this ends.
My heart beats to a rhythm I made up in song.
These words are my lyrics I knew all along.

31. Mermaider

I am known as mermaider I breathe air I breathe sea
I flow through these currents like electricity.
I've seen mythical creatures half human half fish
A Goddess named Athena tame a horse named Pegasus.
I've hit cruise control, swim to these outer limits
No tracking of time, the passing of minutes.
Like time stood still and it got real quiet
You should find this place, I recommend you try it...

32. Tightrope Of Hope

We all have our beliefs, we have our expectations.
We have different views and visions, final destinations.
I could lead you through the darkness, I could show you the light.
The pathway is narrow, to get through we must fight.
In the end of all time, some will not accept truth.
Some they need the facts, scientific mathematical proof.
They need the time to discover, the hidden meaning of things.
They need to wait on their government to see what they may bring.
Nothing at their table, we all have sat alone.
While they are gathering data, tracking devices on your phone.
Just turn off your tv's and stop listening to all the media.
Their deceiving all our minds, just look what they are feeding ya.
They'll leave you lost in illusions, some becoming permanently blind.
Brainwashing the masses one by one, one channel at a time.
Time for action is now, we need more than just talking.
Some claim their woke, some wide awake, while others are sleep walking.

I'll hold on to my faith, and I'll use my God given talents. While I walk this tightrope of hope and try not to lose my balance.

33. A War For The Mind

I'm caught in this spiritual war, trapped in this flesh, trapped in my bones.
So many lost souls trying to find truth, while sifting through all the unknowns.
This social experiment has infected us all, infected us all with group think.
Now their censoring all of us, taking down post, unavailable links.

Social media keeping track, they'll use our words for crucifixions.
It's like an addiction we all have, to want to share all our opinions.
Held hostage by these virtues while trying to use my spiritual gift.
Freedom's not a privilege it's a right we're all born with.

If history repeats itself then just re read, you'll find the proof.
If the pen is mightier than the sword then I'll spread this virus of truth.
We all feel it in our souls, don't fight your brother for all their lies.
The future will view all history as a crime, when will we

rise?

For all future generations that will be silenced what does this teach?
So many died for our constitution, for our rights, our freedom of speech.
This broken system we fight about, they robbed us all, I call that theft.
For these crimes against humanity, their punishment should be death.

We're all fighting with each other, what are we really fighting for?
All this mental noise that's going around I can't take anymore.
You point to the left, you point to the right, who came up with all these directions?
Spreading fear is the real virus, they try to alter all our perceptions.

Lack of true knowledge has you in doubt, so many things that they've kept hidden.
Their evil algorithms, using frequencies on your tell lie visions.
Newscast, comcast, an emergency message about to broadcast.
When the media entered our homes we became

spellbound, the spell was cast.

A warning is a threat and we don't negotiate with terrorists.
We the people are waking up and studying things we all have missed.
I've stared into the abyss for far longer than I care to admit.
The tree of knowledge, just useless information in this bottomless pit.

There's been too much speculation, no certainty of what is real.
We need to get back inside ourselves, it's the only way to heal.
So while the veil is lifted, things being exposed, all things that became evil.
I pray to God for all humanity and stand with we the people.

No matter what your beliefs are or what you find to be true.
The only one who holds the power to change anything would be you.

34. Outlaw

There's a path to the wilderness in the middle you dwell.
One path leads to heaven and one puts you through hell.
One doorway is narrow and one door is wide.
He gives you the choice for you to decide.
He died for our sins by paying our dues.
A fork in the road now it's my time to choose.
The trail I was on I have felt his wrath.
 I pray for protection from the aftermath.
He walks by my side just letting me be.
The roads less traveled I take that for me.
The devil is there he's right on my heels.
Telling me lies and making these deals.
I sit sometimes and stare at the darkness.
Life seems quiet, feels safe, seems harmless.
But I feel like my life is being timed.
I can hear this ticking inside of my mind.
It's hard to change when you've always known.
They way you are from the things you were shown.
I put a smile on my face and try to pretend.
I've fallen down hard but get back up again.
All of my sins have been erased.
By God's never ending love his amazing grace.
If he can change the seasons he can change the wind.
He can save an outlaw like you my friend.

35. Twisting Clocks

The present is here, the future's ahead, inside I start to explore.
I've conjured up thoughts inside my mind, many roads I took before.
I think of things like where were we before we entered earth
Who breathed life into my soul and pushed me through my birth?
Deep in my mind, this voice in the dark, sounds like whispers through the silence.
My faith is in God, my saving grace, who do you look to for guidance?
What doesn't kill you makes you stronger, but first it takes you down.
All the way to the bottom, nowhere left to go but turn around.
Blank pages stare me down to fill, many journals I have kept.
An open book becomes my weapon, that's all that I have left.
My pain is in these pages, I've been torn, I sometimes hide.
Do not inquire into my mind, I am the child lost deep inside.

They want to get to know me, work on chapters to re write.
But they were already written, I close my book, I hold on tight.
As cosmic dust we swirl the abyss, as humans we are transcending.
Through the universe and back, through life and death it is unending.

36. Chaotic Blend

Lost in a swirl of a chaotic blend
Mixing my enemies amongst my friends
Once I learn their rules and then I will send
All of these games they try to amend
While you believe they play pretend
Why do we let this system prevail?
For all of us are subject to fail
They hunt the streets and water we sail
For their opinions we are hauled off to jail
On of them to collect our bail
While going home to more bills in the mail
Where is all the money they eagerly accept
To take their help is to regret
In the end they never forget
To the mansions they live we pay the rent
Taking chunks out my paycheck has left a dent
And all I can do is Vent! Vent! Vent!
While I go home to my tent
And look at mail that is sent
And my money that is meant
Not for me they have spent
On my mind that has went.

www.ingramcontent.com/pod-product-compliance
Lightning Source LLC
Chambersburg PA
CBHW060202050426
42446CB00013B/2959